The Ultimate Audition Book
for Teens Volume XII

III One-Minute Monologues
Just Comedy!

THE ULTIMATE AUDITION BOOK FOR TEENS SERIES

The Ultimate Audition Book for Teens Volume 1:
111 One-Minute Monologues by Janet Milstein

The Ultimate Audition Book for Teens Volume 2:
111 One-Minute Monologues by L. E. McCullough

The Ultimate Audition Book for Teens Volume 3:
111 One-Minute Monologues by Kristen Dabrowski

The Ultimate Audition Book for Teens Volume 4:
111 One-Minute Monologues by Debbie Lamedman

The Ultimate Audition Book for Teens Volume 5:
111 Shakespeare Monologues

THE ULTIMATE SCENE STUDY SERIES FOR TEENS ·

The Ultimate Scene Study Series for Teens Volume 1:
60 Shakespeare Scenes

The Ultimate Scene Study Series for Teens Volume 2:
60 Short Scenes by Debbie Lamedman

THE ULTIMATE MONOLOGUE SERIES
FOR MIDDLE SCHOOL ACTORS

The Ultimate Monologue Book for Middle School Actors Volume 1:
111 One-Minute Monologues by Kristen Dabrowski

The Ultimate Monologue Book for Middle School Actors Volume 2:
111 One-Minute Monologues by Janet Milstein

The Ultimate Monologue Book for Middle School Actors Volume 3:
111 One-Minute Monologues by L. E. McCullough

To order call toll-free (888) 282-2881
or visit us online at www.smithandkraus.com

The Ultimate
Audition Book for Teens
VOLUME XII

• • •

111 One-Minute
Monologues
Just Comedy!

Kristen Dabrowski

YOUNG ACTORS SERIES

A Smith and Kraus Book

A Smith and Kraus Book
Published by Smith and Kraus, Inc.
177 Lyme Road, Hanover, NH 03755
www.smithandkraus.com

First Edition: September 2007
Manufactured in the United States of America
10 9 8 7 6 5 4 3 2 1

Cover and text design by
Julia Gignoux, Freedom Hill Design

ISBN 978-1-57525-580-4
Library of Congress Control Number: 2007934765

To Gene Wilder, Madeline Kahn, Steve Martin,
and all the people who make me laugh.

Contents

Monologues

Introduction

Hello, actors! As a professional actor for fourteen years now, I know how hard the search for the perfect monologue can be. A monologue should be immediate, active, and fun. You shouldn't mind having to say it over and over when you're practicing, auditioning, or performing it. You should be able to relate to it. This is difficult; most plays are written for adults. Where are you supposed to get monologues from then? This book.

Here are some tips on approaching monologues:

1. Pick the monologue that hits you. Trust your instincts. You'll pick the right one!

2. Make the monologues active. What do you want and how do you try to get it?

3. Who are you talking to and where are they? Make sure you make this as clear as possible.

4. Do you get answered or interrupted? Be sure to fill in words in your head for the moments when you are spoken to in the monologue, even if it's a simple yes or no.

5. How do you feel about the person or people you are talking to? For example, you speak a lot differently to your best friend than you do to your math teacher.

6. Notes about stage directions and terminology: The word *beat* or the start of a new paragraph indicates another character speaks or a new idea arises. *Pause* or other stage directions like *shocked* are suggestions, but do not need to be observed absolutely.

Final note: I absolutely encourage you to make strong character choices (how you walk and talk, and so forth). Comedy is best when it's rooted in real feeling, but the energy and character choices are bold. Once you've made character decisions, commit to your choices; don't hold back!

Enjoy!

Kristen Dabrowski

Female Monologues

• • •

THE END OF THE WORLD

LAILA

Did you hear this? I just saw a commercial where they say that video games are a bigger industry now than the movies. How sick is that? At least the movies are social. Like you go to them with your friends or on a date. Well, I guess you can play video games with other people. But don't most people sit alone and, like, try to get to the next level or get the golden cup or whatever?

Plus, this brings up a whole new level of scariness. If video games are such a huge business, it occurs to me that maybe the whole world is being taken over by geeks. I mean, the human race is going to die out completely if this is where we're headed. We are surrounded by geeks alone in their smelly bedrooms playing video games! And these geeks are obviously converting possible normal and cute guys into their evil web of gaming. They don't need human contact. They don't need girls. We are doomed. I am so depressed. Seriously.

LONG LOST

JULIA

Hi! Oh my God. It's been ages since I saw you! How are
you? Oh my God, I can't believe I ran into you! I was saying
to Jessie just the other day, "What ever happened to Melissa?
She went to another school and just disappeared." Hey, your
hair is *so* different. I almost didn't recognize you. It's a little
weird. What made you decide to go with green? And your
eyes are . . . are you wearing contacts?

Um, oh my God, you're not Melissa, are you? Oh my God,
this is so embarrassing! I'm so sorry! I don't know what I
was thinking; I mean, I just really miss her. We were like best
friends. And then she just went poof! You know? And I
thought, "Did I do something to her?" I mean, I always
thought we were best friends, and you just look a *lot* like
her . . .

You're her sister? Oh! I knew it! You totally look similar. So,
anyway . . . uh, tell her I said hi. Not all the other stuff, OK?
Just hi. Oh, and I love the green hair. I was just saying that
'cause, well, you know. She's being a total jerk, and I completely hate her.

So tell her to call me, OK?

SECRETS AND LIES

PARKER

Ella, come in here! Shh! Don't say anything. I have to show you something. But you can't say anything. OK? Swear? OK. Look.

Shh! What did I tell you? Don't say anything. You have to help me figure out what to do. I spilled some nail polish on the rug, so I poured some nail polish remover on it. And then the stain spread and changed the color. So I started looking around and I got some lemon juice from the fridge 'cause the nail polish remover was stinking and it seemed like a good idea, but then the rug turned yellowish-white. So then I started thinking about what would make it brown again, and, I don't know, I guess I'm crazy, but I was desperate, so Dad's shoe polish seemed like a good idea. Anyhow, I've got a huge mess here that just keeps getting worse and worse and Mom and Dad are going to kill me! What should I do?

Chocolate sauce? How in the world would that help? I should have known you'd be too little to help. That doesn't make any sense. Never mind. I'll just tell Mom and Dad you did it.

I was just kidding! Stop crying. Jeez!

HOT

CLAIRE

No, I didn't hook up with him. I don't even like him, Evan! I like you. I *love* you. You know I do. I don't know why you'd say something like that. You really are being paranoid. Look, I danced with my girlfriends, too. You don't think I hooked up with them, do you? So, see? It makes no sense.

I don't know what Shauna told you, but she's lying. OK, I *might* have said, like, months ago that I liked Michael, but that was before I was even dating you. She said I said that last week? Whatever! He's not even my type. I wouldn't do anything to jeopardize what we have. I love you, Evan. I've loved you for, like, weeks now. And nothing's going to stand in our way. Not even Shauna. She's jealous. Well, because she likes Michael, too, and she knows that he's more into me than her. Well, I know that he's into me because . . . well, because he told me *years* ago that he likes blondes, that's why!

You have no right to judge me! I can't help it if I'm really attractive to other men!

SAT

KIKI

But I don't want to babysit. Why do I have to? I have homework to do. Can't I have time to myself? I'm not your
employee. Oh, don't start with the "I gave you life" speech. I
already know what you're going to say. I owe this to you; it's
the least I can do considering all you've done for me . . .
Please, Mom, I'm so sick of taking care of Lily. You have no
idea what she's like when you're not here. A total brat. It's
true! She does everything that you won't let her do. She tries
to push my buttons. She bugs me incessantly. It's insane.
Please, Mom, get someone else to do it. She'll be good for
someone else. I know it's selfish, but I could really use a
night of relaxation. Math class is really stressing me out. You
have no idea how hard algebra is.

Thank you so much! *(Beat.)* What do you mean "I'll get a
babysitter for the *two* of you"? I don't need a babysitter. I'm
not a baby, Mom! That's not what I meant at all. You just
don't understand me. I'm fourteen! God!

UNPREPARED

DELIA

Oh my God. I forgot to put on deodorant today. And I have gym first period! What am I going to do? I can't fake cramps because I did that last week. And old Dorkinhopper has it out for me. I know she's not going to let me get away with sitting out today. I'm screwed! And Tony Macalvy sits next to me in English class. I *love* Tony Macalvy. Love, love, love him! And he's going to think I'm some stinky beast. All because I got a little absentminded this morning. I swear, I have to pay more attention to things! My mom keeps telling me that. I'm always doing things like this. The other day, my mom freaked because I left my bag in the food court at the mall, and we had to drive back. It was still there, thank God. But this is the absolute worst. I swear from this day forward to always concentrate really hard and pay attention to everything around me, everything I have to do.

What class do we have now?

EXHIBIT B-R-A

SUZANNE

What the hell is that? Did—did my rib just come out? I'd feel that, wouldn't I? I mean, I felt some irritation, but . . . Oh my God. It's my bra. The underwire. It came out. I'm just going to pull it out. What do you mean, I can't? I don't care if people see. This *hurts*. I can't exactly walk around for the rest of the day with this thing sticking out of my body. Well, sure I could go do it in the bathroom, but I want to do it now. I'm not going to take my shirt off or anything. Just cover me. God, Inga, you worry too much about what other people think. *I'm* your friend, you should worry about what *I* think. Fine, fine! Just walk about three inches in front of me to the bathroom so nobody can see this thing sticking out of my chest. OK?

(Stands and begins to shuffle forward.) Just calm down. *(Addressing the room in a loud voice.)* OK, everyone, there's nothing to see here! Go about your business. Nothing out of the ordinary going on here! Just two people shuffling awkwardly toward the bathroom. *(Quieter, to Inga.)* What? If we're going to do this subtly, you'd better keep walking.

MISS TAKEN

PEARL

Listen, you bitch. I am going to kill you. I heard about what you did. Don't look innocent! You know what you did. You tried to steal my boyfriend away. He told me. See? You should give it up because he cares about *me*, not you. You're not even his type. Just because he kissed you once at some lame party last week doesn't mean he likes you. Look, we've worked through this, and we are stronger than ever. If you ever, *ever* even get within twenty feet of Ryan, I will rip your lips off. I swear it, you—

Gina Delancey? Well, who is this girl? Gina Landers. Oh. Well. Why didn't anyone tell me? Why didn't you tell me, Gina Landers? You just stood there staring at me. Are you trying to make me look stupid? It's like everyone in school is out to get me.

TARGET

MONIQUE

What? Don't touch me, dork. What is it? Just say it, if you
must. What? Are you trying to be funny? I didn't—*(Looks at
her butt.)* Oh my God, I did. What the hell is it? Chocolate? I
have to go home. I have to change. I can't walk around like
this all day. Oh my God, it's halfway through the day. How
long has it been there? Have I been walking around like this
all day?

No? Are you sure? Hey, wait. How do you know? Have you
been staring at my butt? Are you some kind of pervert?
Don't ever look at me again.

Oh. Thanks for telling me, by the way.

ROTTEN

JOI

Oh! Ouch! My tooth hurts. This one! Ow; it kills! I can't eat my lunch. I'm starving, too. This sucks. No, no. I don't want to tell anyone. What for? I do *not* want to go to the dentist. No way. I hate the dentist. I don't care if I have a cavity; I'm not doing it! I'd rather just let my whole mouth rot.

Look, I just hate the dentist! I don't know the worst that could happen. Maybe he could remove all my teeth. I don't know! I just know that every time I go it's a horrible ordeal. I'm not going to put myself through it. Ow! Ow! That really hurts. Just leave me to curl up and die.

What can the nurse do for me? That's true. I will get out of classes for the rest of the day. But then she'll call my parents and tell them about my tooth. I'm not sure I can risk it. Oooo! Ow! OK! OK! I'm going.

OWNERSHIP

CORAL

You got what on the test? An A? Let me see that! That's not possible. This test was *hard.* You never study. Why did you study for this one? I can't believe *you're* the person who threw off the curve. You.

Come on. You can tell me. Did you cheat? Did you get the answers from someone? Did you look over someone's shoulder?

You studied. You're going to stick with that story. Well, I'm sorry, but I don't believe it! You don't do your homework, and you never put in any effort. It's not fair that you got an A!

What did I get on the test? Well, I got an A-minus. But I studied with my brother, and he took the class last year, so that is *my* A.

REALITY CHECK, PLEASE

VICTORIA

I hate that movie. *Pretty Woman* is so stupid! Like any rich, handsome guy is really going to pick up a prostitute, fix her up, buy her stuff, and marry her. Give me a break. That is never on the planet Earth going to happen! It gives people a false idea of what it's like to be a prostitute. It can't be good or fun and most people just get killed or are, like, junkies.

I am not too serious! I just will not watch that movie. Pick another one, please. *Weekend at Bernie's*? Two guys drag this dead dude all over? If you put some dead guy on a beach, some major stench is going to come off of him. It's ridiculous.

I can't help it if you pick movies that don't make any sense! No! Put that down. *The Breakfast Club*? Like the rich and popular kids would *ever* have anything to do with the freaks and dorks. I can't overlook things like that! Let's just watch *Friday the 13th*. Sure, I can believe that. Have you ever watched the news?

IN THE MOMENT

BRIGITTE

Oh, gross. My sandwich feels wet. I hate sandwiches at lunch. The bread gets all gross. But if I tell my mom that I'll hurt her feelings. Can I have your brownie? Do you want me to starve? Can I borrow some lunch money? My mom won't give me any. She thinks it's nicer to make me a lunch. But she always gives me healthy stuff. I don't want to be healthy. I want to rot my guts. I'll worry about being healthy when I'm old. No, I don't care if I get fat. I won't. I never have. Please, I won't get sick. I've been surviving on preservatives for years now. I eat nothing but sugar if I can help it. If my teeth fall out, I'll get new ones put in. I brush my teeth, dummy; they're not gonna fall out. I'm really not worried about the future. I live in the *now*. Why waste time worrying about what's going to happen when I'm old? Maybe I won't get old. Who knows? So I need to enjoy life right this minute. Give me that brownie, Jeannie. I live on the edge.

SPOOKY

ARIEL

My mom is such a pain. I want to be a sexy cat for Hal-
loween, but she wants me to be completely covered. So I told
her, "I will be covered! I'll wear tights and everything." But
she's like, "No, that's too revealing." So what am I supposed
to do? Go as my grandma or something? I never get to do
anything cool. I always have to do something totally dorky.
Why can't she understand that I want to do something different? I'm getting to an age where I should get to do whatever
I want. Is she trying to destroy my whole high-school experience? Guess what she suggested this year. You won't even
believe it; it's so weird. She thinks I should be a Tootsie Roll.
A big, fat tube with little feet sticking out of the bottom. She
thinks I'm six years old still. No one even likes Tootsie Rolls!
You do? Yeah, but would you dress like one?

See what I mean?

SKINNY GENE

CARI

I think he's dead sexy. I'm serious. I mean look at him! I *like* skinny guys. Gene has a rock-star body. I can't believe you don't see it. It's just as well. I want him for myself. I don't care if I look fat next to him. I mean, as long as he doesn't care. I just think he's incredibly cute. His eyes, I guess, too. I mean, he looks like he's got a secret. A really delicious secret. He sort of smiles with his eyes. Does that sound stupid? It's just that the other day I said hi to him and he said hi and he smiled in this way like he was sort of laughing like he was happy that I said hello to him. He wasn't laughing *at* me; Lila, he was laughing *with* me. I'm sure of it. I think maybe he likes me, too. I can see us getting tattoos together and having little rock-star babies. I'm telling you, Lila, he is gorgeous and he is *mine*.

UNIQUE CRITIQUE

ZOE

I like my big teeth. I think they're cute. I wouldn't change them for all the world. Just because the world of beauty thinks my teeth are flawed doesn't mean I have to think so, too. They're what makes me special. I have a big smile.

You're like this, too. Unique. Your nose is straight and kinda big. It's like classical statues. But it's beautiful and it's *you*. Don't get upset! I was giving you a compliment. Quite honestly. I think you look beautiful. Just like the Madonna in old pieces of art and statues and stuff. No, not that Madonna. Like Mary. Jesus's mother. Haven't you ever seen those things? Well, Mary has a really serene beautiful face all the time, and her nose is just like yours. Really nice. Honestly. I'm not just saying that. I love your nose, and I love my crazy teeth, too.

So, it doesn't bother me that you make fun of them. It doesn't. Everyone who loves me thinks my teeth are perfect, so, basically, you can just take your big nose elsewhere if you don't like them.

DIVA TRIP

MICHELLE

No. I'm not going on the camping trip. There is no way I'm going to sleep on the ground. And pee behind a bush. No way. I need electricity and toilet paper and showers. I won't go. I don't care if I don't bond with the class of whatever. I don't care if I don't graduate! I won't do it. There are bugs and snakes and all kinds of gross things out there.

I have a certain reputation. I need to look a certain way. I'll be honest with you, Mrs. Monteverdi, no one at this school has ever seen me in the morning without makeup. I'm seriously hideous. I'm just telling you this because you need to understand why I don't want to go. This isn't just being a girlie girl. This is a matter of life and death. My whole life will fall apart if I go on this camping trip. Why is this trip so important? I'm sorry, but it just sounds dumb. Think about it: if anyone gets hurt, the school will totally get sued. I'm just thinking of you, really. It's just not a good idea.

That's my *real* reason for not wanting to go. I don't want to get hurt. I don't want to sue the school. My dad's a lawyer, Mrs. Monteverdi. Don't you see how this trip is a huge mistake?

TRICK OR TREAT

BRENDA

I can't eat it. Not even a bite. No! Stop trying to tempt me!
I'm serious. You're not being nice. I *don't* need to eat more.
Please. I'm trying to give up sugar. So no cakes or cookies or
brownies. Yeah, *ever*. So? That does not make me a boring
person. It makes me a healthy person. Why are you trying to
corrupt me? This is the *first* day of my diet—no, not diet.
Lifestyle change. Don't ruin it for me.

Whatever. Give it to me. You are a horrible person. I just
want you to know that. You're ruining my life. Now give me
that fork. No, I'm going to eat the whole thing. If I'm going
to go off my diet, I'm going whole hog. No pun intended.

OUTCAST

KATE

I can't go to school like this. Everyone's going to mock me.
Look at the size of me! I can't even fit into my clothes. I have
to wear Dad's pants.

I wish I were coordinated! This is your fault, you know. I got
your awkward, uncoordinated genes. I can't believe I fell
down the stairs and broke my tailbone! Who would believe
they'd give me a cast for breaking my butt! I am, literally, a
foot wider than I was before. This cast is huge! I do not look
like Jennifer Lopez. Don't be stupid. I broke my ass. I look
like an idiot.

Oh, God, I really can't go to school! It hurts to walk, Mom.
Please? Fine! *(Walks away like she's got a huge load in her
pants.)* Don't laugh, Mom! That's it! I'm *not* going!

REFLECTION

CARMEN

Is anything stuck in my teeth? Hold on, I have to look before we go inside, just in case Ethan is working. *(Bears her teeth.)* I have some pesto stuck between my front teeth. Why didn't you tell me? *(Bears her teeth again and digs between her front teeth with her fingernail.)* Is it gone? I think it is. Anything else in there? *(Makes some crazy faces to check the rest of her teeth.)*

OK. Let's go in. Is it me or is everyone looking at me? That girl is pointing at me. And laughing! You don't think . . . I didn't . . . Did they—Oh my God, they saw me checking my teeth in the window. We have to go now. I don't care if you want ice cream! I can never come here again. We have to go—*now*! Ethan? Are you kidding? That's the last thing on my mind. If he's here, I'll just die!

ROUGH

BELINDA

Why don't you want to hold my hand? Is it because we're in public? Because I think that's weird. Why is PDA considered so wrong? It's perfectly natural. I like it when I see people holding hands and kissing. It's cute.

Are you ashamed of me or something? You can like me when no one is looking, but when other people are around—

My hands are dry? My skin? Well, yeah. It's winter. That grosses you out? You like girls with nice hands. Well, I don't have nice hands so you'd better get used to it. I have better things to do than to paint my nails. Now hold my hand or we're through. It's not as if your hands are silky smooth, you know.

THE QUEEN IS DEAD

EVIE

You're not a princess. I hate to tell you that, but it's true.
You should really take that crown off. The other kids are
going to make fun of you when you get to school. Seriously.
Mom, this isn't cute. The other kids are going to be mean to
her. Kids are mean to anyone who seems different from
them. She's walking around with a cape and a crown all the
time. It's weird. It's not normal. It's not!

I'm trying to help! Here's an idea. Maddie, why don't you
pretend you're a princess in disguise as a regular girl?
Princess Maddie wants to go to school to play with other
children, but her dad, King Dave, won't let her go. So every
morning she dresses up like a regular girl and sneaks out of
the castle. And no one at school knows her true identity. It's
a secret.

Mom, you might want to start taking notes. I am such a
genius, even I can't stand it.

UNDERTOW

MORGAN

No. I'm sorry, but no. I can't tell you why. I just can't go. I can't! I-I-I never tell anyone—I've never told—OK! OK! I'm scared. I can't go because I'm afraid of the ocean. I just think about all the things that could happen. I could get stung by a jellyfish or an electric eel or eaten by a shark or I could drown—

You don't swim? You just lie on the beach? Oh. Well. You're not just saying that? Could we sit really far from the water? I sort of feel like the ocean is trying to pull me in. I know it doesn't make sense, but that's what I think. OK. I guess I'll go.

But what if I get skin cancer? That could happen. No. No. Never mind. I'm going to stay home. I hate summer.

GROW UP

JACKIE

Mom, don't wear that. Yeah, it's in, but it's not for you.
Well, yeah, you wore that when you were younger, but that's
just the point. But when was that? Forty years ago? Twenty?
Well, that's a really long time. These are young people
clothes. People your age shouldn't wear spandex ever. It's just
not appropriate. No offense. It doesn't matter if it's comfort-
able. You look sort of pregnant. You shouldn't wear leggings.
Even to the grocery store—*especially* to the grocery store.
People go to the grocery store.

Where did you get those anyway? Are those mine? Mom,
you stretched them all out! Now I can't wear them anymore.
I need new ones now. We have to go to the mall. But you
need to change first. Don't you have a sensible skirt in your
closet? Some jeans that come up to your belly button? I
know, I don't like that look either, but it's better than this.

IN NEUTRAL

MADELINE

Uh, that's OK. I don't need to. Not today. I've got a lot to do. Yeah, I guess it would be OK with me if I never learn to drive. I'm not sure I really want to drive. I can just keep getting driven around by you and Mom. What's so wrong with that? We've been doing well like that for a long time now.

Dad, it just scares me. I can't tell how hard to press the pedals or how far to turn the wheel. It's just horrible. I'd rather not do it. I promise I'll study really hard so I can hire a chauffeur after you're dead, OK? So let's just forget about this driving thing, all right?

TOO ADORABLE

RILEY

What? You don't love me? You. Don't love. Me. You don't love me. You don't love me? I know I keep saying it! Because I can't believe it. I am so lovable. It's actually ridiculous how lovable I am. I am totally, completely adorable. Why don't you love me? I just want to know. Do you have any history of mental instability in your family?

Wow. This is just so surprising. Every boyfriend I ever had told me he loved me practically even before he knew my name. You're different from every other guy I've ever met. I'm, like, that girl you take home to your mother or something. Every guy I've ever known has thought we'd get married and live happily ever after, and *I* had to break up with *them*. This is such a relief. Wow. I'll see you around, I guess. This is fantastic. Thank you so much!

THINGS I NEVER WANT TO SEE

LOLA

Why are you walking around in a towel? Put some clothes on! Oh my God, boys are so stupid. Mom, why are you doing his laundry? I *know* he has nothing to wear, but that's because he waited for you to do his laundry! You never do mine. Why do you do his? Because he's a boy? What year is it anyway? This is such a double standard! Look at it this way, Mom. No one's going to marry a filthy slob, and that's what you're raising here. He's disgusting! And now he's sitting on the couch in a towel.

Mom, I didn't want to say this, but I'm scared. Towels are . . . not secure. Things could happen. It could slip or get caught in a door. I don't want to see my brother naked. It would scar me for life. Make him learn how to do his laundry and make him stay in his room. Please, Mom! You never do anything for me!

DISILLUSIONED

ESMÉ

(Wearing very trendy clothes.) Have you always listened to jazz music, Dad? It's kind of like old-man music, so I was wondering how you got into it. Did you listen to pop or rock or anything when you were younger? You liked what? Culture Club? Boy George?? Are you serious? I used to respect you, Dad. Seriously.

You're kidding. Tell me you're kidding. You used to dress like him? Didn't he wear dresses? You had long hair and wore a hat. And eyeliner. No. This is a joke, right? Very funny! You can stop now.

Come on! Stop it! I'm going to have nightmares tonight. Does Mom know about this?

She dressed like Madonna? This story keeps getting worse and worse. I really hope I repress this memory. You in make-up has me totally freaked out!

A STRONG WOMYN

HOLLY

I don't need help. I'm fine. I can carry my suitcases on my own. I said that you don't need to help me! Put that down. Put it down! I know you're trying to be helpful, but I don't need your help. You need to listen.

I can accept help. I just think that guys think girls are helpless, and I hate that. I can take care of myself. I just don't want anyone to think I'm weak. I'm not weak. I'm strong. I can do whatever I put my mind to. I can carry six suitcases. It's not a problem.

(Annoyed.) Yes, I know it's a stereotype for girls to carry too many suitcases. I couldn't help it. It could rain or it could snow or it could be warm—how am I to know what kind of weather we're going to have? Stop judging me! *(Begins to storm off. Beat. Returns.)* OK, fine. Carry my suitcases if it will make you happy.

TAN

JANINE

Am I orange? Some girl on MySpace said I was orange. I'm not, right? She's just jealous, right? I tan. I'm tan. Everybody tans. If I didn't tan, people would say I was pale. You just can't win. Of course, I'm not bothered by it. Who the hell is she? I bet she's not that pretty either. I looked her up. Her pictures online looked OK, but maybe it's not even her. Besides, it's what's inside that's important, right? She's all cold and icy inside. I'd rather be me. I like who I am. I like how I look. I like my tan.

(Beat.) So, she's wrong, right? My tan is nice, right? Not that I care what she thinks, but you'd tell me the truth if I was, right? Who the hell does that old, ugly bitch think she is anyway? At least I'm a good person.

AGONY

CAROLINE

Why do guys wait before calling? Why can't he call right away? I hate waiting. I don't get it either. It's nice when someone calls you the next day. I mean, Brian bugged me for hours at Melanie's party. Kept asking if he could call me, asking for my number. So I finally give it to him, and this is what I get? Now he has the power. It's wrong. I liked it better when I was the one in control.

I don't know if I like him. I know I don't *dis*like him. I like him, you know, but I don't know if I *like* him. So I thought I'd go out with him and see what happens. But I'm going to hate him if he doesn't call. Because then . . . I don't know. It makes me feel like crap when . . . It'll feel like he rejected me if he doesn't call. And I should be the one rejecting him! He begged for my number, Sarah. This is ridiculous. Let's go to the mall. I need ice cream.

YOUNG AT FACE

MARTHA

What? What do you mean? Well, OK. Why are you telling me that? I'm not in seventh grade. I'm a junior in high school. I'm here to take the SAT. You thought I was in *seventh* grade? What are the seventh graders doing here on the weekend? They take the SAT, too? If they're gifted? I guess it's good that I seem "gifted," whatever that means. But seventh graders are only, like, twelve! I know I'm not that tall, but, God . . . Wow. This sucks. Would it help if I wore my hair up? Or if I wore makeup? It's just that it's so early, so I just came in my pajamas. God, I can't believe I look twelve.

Hey, that's true. Maybe when I'm sixty I'll look like I'm forty or something. That will be good, I guess. Hey, thanks! I feel better.

I think.

EXTREME MEASURES

BETH

I know this is weird for me to say, but I think I'm going to try out for track. I know I'm out of shape. Thanks for the totally obvious observation. I'm fat. But that's the whole point. I have to do something about it. Believe me, I don't want to do it. I wish I was skinny, and I didn't have to exercise, but that's not the case. Our whole family is overweight. I just want to stop the cycle here and now. I know how your feet hurt all the time, and you get tired. The same stuff happens to me, too, and I'm only fifteen. But I don't want to have heart problems and diabetes. I want to be healthy. So that's why I'm doing this. It's going to be incredibly embarrassing and horrible, I'm sure, both because no one wants to see a fat girl run, but also because I *am* out of shape, but this is something I have to do. So I hope you'll be supportive about this.

Thanks, Mom. Will you take me shopping now for the biggest sports bra we can lay our hands on? I'm going to need another kind of support, too.

SPOKEN FOR

GLORIA

But what about—I think—I was watching a news conference the other day— Don't Republicans do the same thing? Oh my God. You never let me get a whole sentence out! What is your problem? Of course I'm ignorant. It's because you never let me finish an entire thought. How can I be an intelligent, thoughtful person—

Aaaah! Never mind. I'm going to go talk to the cat. The cat lets me finish a sentence. Yes, I finished a sentence just then, but when I want to—Aaaah! Don't you hear yourself? Don't you hear what you're doing to me? Where are you going? Why do you run away when I want to have a conversation? When I want to tell you what I think? You are in love with your own voice.

I know I'm talking to myself! I'm really fun to talk to. You'd know if—

Oh, never mind. I give up!

MY HUMPS

DAWN

(Shaking her leg.) Um, Jenny? Could you get your dog? It's kind of on me. On my . . . leg. It's on my leg. Please? Can you come in here? I can't get it off. It's stuck. And it's pretty gross. Please! I need help! He won't get off. I can't get him off! Heeeeeeeeeelp!

(Leg still.) Thank you. Thank you! Where were you? Your dog was, like, having sex with my leg. I'm so humiliated. I need to go home now. I'm never coming back here. Sorry. I feel so . . . violated!

JUICY

MILLIE

I wish I could go to some desert island where people didn't gossip. Life would be so much easier. I just don't want to know that Marsha Lipman tongue kissed her dog. Whether it's true or not! I just don't want to have that kind of information. Or that Dennis Rector wears girl's underwear. I'd just rather exist in the world without knowing these things. There are certain topics that are just not my business.

No, I don't want to know about Raymond Hartigan. I don't care if it's juicy or not. No, Regina! I don't want to hear it!

(Beat.)

OK, fine. What is it? I changed my mind. I mean, I don't want to know, but I do. Know what I mean? So tell me already!

NATURE

CELIA

I love flowers. They are so pretty. It's so sad that we never see them that much in the city. Not real flowers like this. Not flowers actually in the ground. Only cut flowers that are probably old. A couple of years back, my mom had this boyfriend who bought her roses. They were really nice. But they didn't smell like anything. And they died in two days. It was sad. They were pretty while they lasted. The guy lasted for a little longer than the flowers, but not by a lot.

Anyhow, this is amazing. All these fresh, beautiful flowers in every color in the rainbow. I just want to take this all in. *(Takes a really deep breath.)* I could just—*(Sneezes.)* Oh! Excuse me. I was going to say that I could just—*(Sneezes.)* I think I could live here and—*(Sneezes.)* be totally happy. *(Sneezes.)* But now that I think about it, I want to get out of here before I die! *(Sneezes.)* I can't wait to get back to the city!

RELEASE

C. J.

Know what? I can't be quiet! I don't want to be quiet any more! I'm sick of it! I'm sick of being polite—the good little girl. I want to scream and yell! I want to be unreasonable! Is there a problem with that? Why is it so awful for me to be the tiniest bit outside of the norm. Other kids are so rebellious, so bad. And I have such a small, little box to live in. It's constricting! Don't you see what you're doing to me? So I'm going to yell right here, right now in the supermarket. I want to be free! I want to be happy!

Aaaaaaahhhhhh! There. I did it. So there. And now I feel . . . silly. I hate you. Why did you let me do that?

IT'S A MYSTERY

CATHERINE

I don't care. I like these shows. I know they're silly. So? You like silly things, too. You don't think that watching films where two hundred people get shot but not the hero are normal? That's ridiculous. So just shut up and go away. You have to pay attention to these shows, Jimmy, so you can tell who did it. Oh, Jesus. I know the sister of the librarian did it. It's always the least likely person. But that's not the point. I want to see *why* she did it and how the detective figures it out. Don't you have to go pick your nose or something?

Shhh! The guy with the moustache is on a bicycle with a package! This is the best part!

ROCKS DON'T ROCK

FRANCESCA

Ooooh. Ooooooh! This is awful! Ooooh, I can't stand this!
Why do they put us through this torture? I can't bear it anymore! I'm going to break. I'm going to just explode into a
tiny green globule. I cannot take another second of earth sci-
ences. I don't care about rocks. I don't care! I don't know
how I'm supposed to write a paper about them. Ten pages?
What in the world can I say? What does he want from me?
Here's what I have so far. Plate Tectonics by Francesca Halla-
day. How do you like it? Do you think I'll get an A? It's just
not possible to live through this class. I am seriously going to
perish. Every day Mr. Gray turns off the lights to show us
slides of rocks and diagrams of I don't even know what. It's
like he's daring me to fall asleep. I would take— God, anything!— French thirty times over rather than take this class
once. And you know how I hate French.

Can't we all just be happy there is an earth and leave it at that?

FOLLOW THE LEADER

JILL

Come on, guys. We need to practice. I've got some new moves that I think you're gonna like. I took them off of a video I saw last night? Come on! Get up! What do you mean you don't want to do it? We are in a position to be a huge success, to be, like, famous, at the talent show this year. We could be legends! Or we could suck ass and be a laughing-stock. Which do you want to be? No! These moves are good. They are. I stole them directly off of the best videos on MTV. Justin Timberlake, stuff like that. If we can pull this off . . .

I seriously don't get you guys. I hate you. You are totally let-ting me down! I can't believe this. Never speak to me again. No, don't, Brianna! No! You can't even apologize. I hate you forever.

Well, OK. I forgive you. Now watch this move. It is going to blow your mind!

PICTURE UN-PERFECT

ALISON

Mom! This is horrible! I can't use this. This picture cannot appear in the yearbook. I will die. I look like a fat pig in this picture! This is the most humiliating day in my life. Don't lie to me. I don't look pretty. Now I can't believe anything you say ever again. You've probably been lying to me all my life. You don't love me. You don't care about me. If you did, you'd do something about this picture! I don't know; call the school or something. Tell them I need a reshoot. This is about posterity. This picture is going to last a lifetime. People are going to have the yearbook on their shelves their whole lives. This year is going to be horrible enough, but every time there's a reunion, I'll have to relive this humiliation. People will be all like, "Remember this girl? What a fat slut! She looks like a huge hog! I bet she weighs, like, four hundred pounds now." I will *never* live this down. I may as well die now.

Please, Mommy, can't you call the school and get them to retake the pictures? Please? Or maybe we can hire a professional photographer. Please?

DRESSED

KYLIE

I want to be a nurse. I want to help people. No, I don't want to be a doctor. Too much school. Plus, doctors' outfits are not hot. Nurses' outfits are too hot! They are! They're, like, an icon of hotness. That *does* make sense, stupid. Show what you know.

No, I've never been to the hospital. I'm healthy. I'm a healthy person. Why would I go to the hospital? I know I want to be a nurse from TV. Oh, yeah. I guess they do wear those scrubs. But isn't there a choice? Couldn't I wear the cute little dress instead? The doctor's office I went to as a little girl had an old lady there who wore the dress. I'll just work in a doctor's office instead. So there! You think you know everything.

UNDONE

BABS

You let him in? You said I would be down in a minute?
What were you thinking? Dad, I just woke up! My hair is a
mess. I haven't taken a shower. I'm hideous. Tell him I'm not
here. Tell him I'm sick. Tell him—I don't care what you tell
him! I can't believe you put me in this position. This is
embarrassing. He's just going to have to wait for an hour.
That's how long he's going to have to wait.

You don't understand at all, Dad. It *does* matter. If he sees
me looking like this, he'll never speak to me again. Oh,
don't. Please. Don't tell me that if he doesn't speak to me
again then he's not worthy of me, blah blah blah. It's just the
facts. It's how life is. I didn't make up the rules. Men are
shallow, Dad. Everyone knows that.

No, you cannot sit down there and talk to him! Leave him
alone. You've done enough damage. He'll just have to wait
until I figure out what to do with my hair.

STANDARDS

CARLA

Oh no. No. We're over. It's over. It's done. I'm sorry. It's . . . I can't believe you'd have to ask. Isn't it obvious? It's . . . your locker. It's filthy. Messy. Disorganized. Someone who has a messy locker has a messy room and a messy life. It's a sign of a disordered mind. I can't be with someone like that. It's just asking for disaster.

Look, I know it's not exactly my business, since we're not together anymore, but maybe you should try to do something about this. Before it's too late. Before you're living alone in a cockroach-infested apartment, and you get killed when too many magazines fall over and crush you. That's where you're headed.

I'm just trying to be helpful. I thought maybe we could try being friends, but I can see that's not going to work, either. That's OK with me. I was just trying for your benefit; I think I could be good for you. Well, see you around. And good luck. Really, think about that magazine thing. It's a terrible way to go.

AT HOME

JOLENE

(In a strong regional accent, such as southern or New York.)
Oh my God. Your accent is crazy! Where are you from? Oh
my God! Keep talking! That is hysterical. You sound so
bizarre. I'm sorry, but I can't get over it. You're Canadian?
Weird!

I don't have an accent. I sound like everybody else. *You're*
the one that sounds different.

What are you talking about? People on TV? I never paid
attention to how they sound. Listen, let me give you a hint.
Try to get rid of that accent or everyone's going to make fun
of you. Stick with me; I'll help you get rid of it. Before you
know it, you'll sound just like everyone else!

COOKIN'

MARISOL

You always ask us to help out with things around the house, and when I do, you complain. I cooked for you. I did my best. I was trying to help. I can't believe— Is it so bad? What's wrong with it? I followed the recipe really carefully. I did everything it said. It's not my fault if it's not good.

It's awful? Don't be mean. How can it be? I don't understand. No, I didn't taste it. I didn't think it would be hygienic if I tasted it. I was really careful about following the recipe; I thought it would be fine. Actually, I thought it would be really good. The recipe sounded good. There's a garlic in it and— Well, yeah, I put a whole garlic. Two, actually. It said "two garlic," see? Well, two cloves. What's a clove? Just the little bit? Not the whole thing? Oh.

It took me two hours to make this damn meal! I can't believe it. Why didn't you ever teach me what a clove of garlic was? Don't worry; I'm never cooking again. I'll never try to help out around the house again!

(Runs out.)

WEDDING DAY

PAULETTE

(Laughs loudly.) Holy crap! This is the worst music I've ever heard. Jesus, Mary Jane, you know it's true. Excuse me for being the only one brave enough to say so. Nobody heard me. Chill out!

Well, I don't know what kind of music I'd have at a wedding; I just know it wouldn't be *this*. It doesn't matter if the bride and groom like it. They should have a little shame. Or taste. I am behaving myself! What's so bad about speaking my mind? Honestly, everyone talks about free speech and communication, but no one actually wants to hear it.

Oh, hi, Cousin Cecilia! We are having *such* a good time. Yeah. Thanks for inviting us. Mary Jane isn't crazy about the band, but *I'm* having a really good time. She really has no manners. You look gorgeous, by the way. OK, bye!

Ow! What did you hit me for?

FREAK SHOW

GOLDIE

OK, girl. Get out there and be a superstar. A supermodel! A glamorous babe. You know you've got it. Go flaunt it! You've been waiting your whole life for this moment—a chance to be seen by the best modeling agencies in the country. Don't be nervous! You can do this. You were *born* to do this! After all, why else would God make you six feet tall and one hundred and twenty pounds? There's no other reason; it's freakish! I mean that in a good way. Like, one in a billion girls look like you. It's like a guy being six foot nine and fast. He just has to be a basketball player. You're genetically built for this. All you have to do now is sashay down that runway toward your dreams. Reach for the brass ring. No, no, there's not actually a brass ring.

Oh! You're next! You can do this, Lindsey. Go get 'em, tiger!

She's doing great, right? I am so proud of— Oh! Oh God! Oooo. That's gotta hurt. Right into the audience. I guess genetics are nothing if you can't walk in heels.

DEMENTED

HEIDI

I can't believe I like you. I'm not supposed to. No one else I know gets along with their mother. You're just so easy to get along with. How can I possible rebel when you're so reasonable, and you agree with me all the time?

Well, I know we're similar. We think the same. That's the worst part. We both like musicals. You like my friends. We like the same movies. We even like the same foods! It sucks! What's wrong with me? What's wrong with you? I should want to date twenty-five-year-olds and get drunk on the weekends. And *you* should try to put me in a nunnery or a German boarding school or something.

OK. Maybe not. But we do have a weird relationship. Thanks to you, I have nothing to talk to my friends about. I'm not having a normal teenage experience, and it's all your fault.

Oh my God! Is this our first fight? Excellent!

GREAT

AUDREE

Look, I'm going to have to tell you this right now. I'm going to beat you. I beat everyone. I'm the best athlete I know. So I hope you can handle that.

I'm not being cocky. I'm being truthful. I just told you because I don't want your feelings to be hurt later on. A lot of guys get uptight about a girl beating them. And I don't want to be associated with someone who's insecure about his masculinity. That's the thing. People look at me, and they think I'm a total bitch. Guys especially. But I'm just self-confident. And honest. Why should I pretend to be less than I am?

So, are we going to bowl or not? I can see you're scared. Why don't we just pretend that I'm too tired to bowl, and we'll grab a hamburger. Just know that I would have beaten you.

WELL SAID

SHEILA

(With a lisp.) Stho, Sthacey, Sthawn is completely amazthing. We met at the sthore this sthummer, and it wasth true love right from the sthart. I sthwear. We sthpent stho much time together. We were, like, instheparatble. And my Aunt Amy was awesthome about it. Sthe really let me do whatever I wanted. I would tan every day, and sthee Sthawn every night.

But I have no idea what to tell my mom. I've avoided her for, like, a day now, but it'sth getting impossthible to keep thisth up. But if sthe findsth out about Sthawn and what I did thisth sthummer, I'm dead. Sthe'll kill me. I might get away with not telling her about my boyfriend, but there'sth no way I can hide thisth tongue piercthing for much longer. What sthould I do, Sthacey?

DON'T HATE ME
BECAUSE I'M BEAUTIFUL

SHANTI

I am so cute. I can't even believe it! I look amazing in this skirt. I love it! Do you love it? I don't know what happened to me this year. I just woke up one day, and I was so damn cute!

Why should I pretend I think I look terrible when I don't? That doesn't make sense. Ooooooh. If I pretend I think I look bad, then when people say I look good, I can pretend to be all surprised and flattered. Let me practice. Tell me I look good.

(Dramatically.) Who *me*? Oh, stop. You are just saying that. I do not look gorgeous!

You're right! I'll get even *more* compliments that way! I'm the kind of girl people want to hate, but they can't. Because I'm so sweet.

DOLL

LALA

Dani, want to come over to my house? I have a plan of what we can do today. I was going through my stuff because my mom wants me to throw things out, and I got the best idea. Let's play Barbies. I haven't done that in so long! Come on, it will be fun. It was fun when we were little! Why wouldn't it be fun now? It will be more fun because everybody's not doing it. We'll be original.

Well, sure, we'll be weird. So what? I *loooove* being weird. You know you want to. You do. All the cool kids are doing it. OK, they're not, but they would if they were creative enough to think of it. Come on. Pleeeeeeeeeease? It'll be like it was when we were six. Only now we know Ken's gay so instead of them going on dates, Barbie can just tell him all of her problems. It will be excellent.

Come on, pleeeeeease? Yay! Thanks, Dani!

APPLY

WILLA

I don't know what I would do with a million dollars or what person, dead or alive, I'd like to meet or even why I think I should be accepted! I have no interesting life experiences. Nothing has ever happened to me, and I have no brilliant ideas. All I can think of is crap that everyone else in the world writes. I don't have an original bone in my body!

I just have to get this done. I keep waiting for inspiration to strike. I can't say anything about world peace—it will make me sound like a Miss America reject! I'm just not a mover and shaker. That's not me. I'm a get-the-job-done, follow-the-rules kind of gal. This just isn't me! OK. I think I just have to try to be original. Catch their attention. How does this sound?

I would buy guitars for the homeless if I had a million dollars. I'd like to meet . . . the most boring person in the world so I never become like them. I don't know what it all means; I'm just desperate! I could use some encouragement here!

HEALTHY

NOLA

(Sitting.) I'm telling you, running is the best thing in the world. It's changed my entire life. I've lost twenty pounds and done two marathons. I'm totally in shape. I feel great! I can't even describe it. It's true what they say about endorphins kicking in when you run. You get this total rush of energy and excitement after about fifteen minutes. You should really try it. We'll run together sometime! I get up before school and do it most days. Want to meet me at six tomorrow morning? It'll be fun.

Give it a try. Would I lie to you? It's really transformed my life. I've never felt better, and I've never felt better about myself. Plus, it can't hurt to be healthy.

(Stands.) Oh! That's the bell. Gotta get to next period. *(Limps away. Turns back.)* Oh, my leg? I just pulled my groin last week. It's fine. A little pain never hurt anyone.

Of course I still run. It's healthy!

Male Monologues

· · ·

THE CHAMP

DMITRI

One more. Are you training for this or not? Do you want to win or not? So, drink it! One more raw egg won't kill you. No, eggs are pasteurized; you won't get salmonella. It didn't kill Rocky, did it? Of course it didn't. No, he didn't talk like that because of eating eggs. He talked like that from being hit in the face too many times. But that's not going to happen to you! You're a champion! Sure, sure, I guess he was a champion, too, but you're not going to let people hit you in the face. That's just stupid. Just use your survival instincts. It won't be a problem.

No, you won't break any bones. This is *boxing* not *football*. Well, you could break your nose, but that's cartilage, not bone. Don't worry. They'll just set it again. Hey, why are you getting so jumpy? Owen Wilson has had his nose broken lots of time, and girls still like him. Girls *love* scars and broken bones and stuff. Yes, they love broken cartilage, too. So drink up!

No! You can't just do track this semester. Come on. Don't be a chicken!

WISE GUY

HOWIE

Um, Jenny. We're about to be in the same school. So. We need to talk. There are some things you need to know. See, high school is pretty tough. So I've had to do some things, some pretty clever things if you ask me, to get by. It would be best for you if you didn't blow my cover. I told people we were rich. Really rich. I get off the bus in front of that big white house on the corner of Greenstone, you know? I told people Dad's a drug dealer. I mean, I told them about the jewelry store, but that's just a front. Get it? Then no one bothers me, and everyone wants to be my friend. It's cool. So you have two choices. You can either go along with the story, or you can pretend we're not related. Which is it going to be?

It's not stupid! People believe it. They've believed it for a year now. They have! No one's laughing behind my back. Dad *could* be a drug dealer if he wanted to. It doesn't even matter if he looks like one or not. No one's ever going to meet him. No one's going to knock on the door at the white house because I told them that we had vicious guard dogs trained to attack *anyone* who's not in our family. It's a genius plan! So are you in or out?

THE GYM

REX

Um, dude, do you need to, uh, grunt so much while you work out? It's really distracting. It sound like, well, it sounds like you're on the toilet, if you get my drift. You sound like you've got a problem. You're getting all the wrong attention. You want people to check you out 'cause you look good, not 'cause you sound like you're having a baby. And it's kind of rude. I'm trying to concentrate on my sets, and there's a guy next to me who's groaning like a mating tortoise. That might sound weird to say, but I heard mating tortoises at the zoo one time, and I can tell you that's exactly what you sound like. So I'd really appreciate it if you'd cut it out.

(Backing up in fear as if the other guy suddenly stood up and he's huge.) Know what? Forget I ever said anything. I was trying to be helpful. But, uh, upon further consideration, I think your grunting sounds like music. Beautiful, beautiful music. So I'll just go way over there and finish my workout, OK?

SMOOTH

ANDRE

Yeah. Do you like it? I did it for the swim team. It's cool, right? Shaved my entire body. So I'll be faster in the water. It takes me, like, forty-five extra minutes in the shower, but it's worth it. Plus, it drives my sister crazy. We share a shower, and she's always screaming at me that she's got to do her hair and she's going to pee herself if I don't get out of the bathroom. It's hysterical.

To be honest, it's getting kind of boring. I never realized how much time it takes. I mean, it takes *ages*. My skin is all puckered when I get out of the shower. But if you think it's sexy . . . I do not have stubble! I just shaved this morning! Aw, damn. I can't believe this. I'm quitting the swim team. I can't deal with this. I mean, I'm a *man*, right? I shouldn't have to do this. I can't believe I already have stubble!

MY IDOL

PAUL

I'm not gay! I have that poster not because I'm in love with that guy, but because I want his body. Not like that! You are such an idiot. It's, like, inspiring. Someday I'm going to look like that. I may be skinny now, but I am going to lift weights until I look like that guy. I'm serious! Look, if Schwartzenegger can do it, so can I. Do you know that he was skinny like me when he was my age? If you work hard enough, anything's possible. I'm already up to twenty-five pushups in a row. OK, that may not be that good, but three weeks ago I couldn't do nearly that many. If I keep up at this rate, my veins will be sticking out of my bulging biceps by Christmas. You won't even recognize me. But I'll give you a hint. I'll be the guy with a bunch of hot girls hanging all over him.

TASTE

NAT

Do you know that when I was a kid I had this thing for eating pencil erasers? I did. Know what else? I still do. They taste awesome. There are so many things people tell you not to eat that are delicious. You know how there are some people who have to smell everything, like markers? I like to taste things, or I did when I was a kid. And some things are actually good. I mean, why is it normal to eat Cheez Doodles, which have, like, no natural ingredients, and it's not normal to eat paste? Paste is sweet. And Play-Doh is salty. And chalk is good, too, but it's hard to eat. It's really . . . hard and sort of grainy. I'm not crazy. Try a pencil eraser. Try it! Go on, it's not going to kill you. I've eaten about a million on them. Just try it.

See? What did I tell you? Awesome, right? It is not gross! Man, you are missing out. You've got to expand your mind a little. You're too conventional. You're missing out. I mean, paste would blow your mind. It's better than cake. I swear.

IN THE DARK

SPENCE

You told me I could paint my room any color I wanted. Well, I want black! You don't understand. I *want* it to be dark. It's where I sleep, right? It's supposed to be dark. I want to give it a nice atmosphere. Jeremy has a black bedroom, and it looks excellent. Look, I'm trying to express myself. I am a rock guy. This is who I am. I'm not you. I'm not going to make my room pale yellow or anything. And you *told* me I could do whatever I wanted with it. You can't take it back. You said it. So what if I have to paint it again before we move? Fine. I'll worry about that when it happens. I *am* sure this is what I want. I want a black bedroom.

What do you mean *no*? You're a liar, you know that? Fine! I'll go to my room. But I'm going to sit in the dark. My room's going to be black one way or another!

NICE

WILL

I just told this girl that she had a stain on her pants, and she went completely nuts on me. I was just trying to be helpful. I swear, girls are so nuts. I mean, if a person is clearly trying to help you, why would you attack them? Then she had the nerve to ask me to switch clothes with her. Like I would do that after she called me a pervert! She said I was a pervert for looking at her butt, but, excuse me, there's a huge stain on it. Most people would just laugh at her and not say anything. I was being *decent*. Nice.

No, I didn't switch clothes with her! I'm not going to walk around all day with girl's jeans on with a big brown stain on the butt. No way!

Well, yeah. She did want to get in my pants. Good point! You are smart, Jason. I like the way you think.

TWINKLE TOES

IRA

Mom, I have to tell you something. I want to be a professional tap dancer. And I don't even know if there's any such thing anymore. But that's what I want. And I thought I ought to come out and tell you. I know you never thought I'd be a tap dancer, and this probably ruins your dreams for me, but I hope you'll think it over and understand that this is what I want to be happy. So I'm going to quit soccer and take more lessons, if I can. I just know that this is the only thing that will make me happy. I've tried to deny it for a long time, but I just can't hold it in any longer. I can't pretend that I'm like the other kids who want to play sports or video games. But don't worry about me. I know this will be a hard life, but if I'm doing what I want, I know I'll be happy. Who knows? Maybe I'll get my own TV show and be hugely famous. Maybe tap dancing will become really popular again. I don't know. But please support my decision and accept me for who I am. I am a tap dancer.

VIEW FROM THE BENCH

FREDDY

I can't play this game? Why not? Just let me in once. What harm could it do? Why are you laughing? I'm not *that* bad. Am I? I'm *that* bad? So bad I could lose the game for the team if I go into the game *once*? Is everyone laughing at me? Why didn't anyone tell me? I had no idea I was a walking disaster area. I mean, I knew I wasn't good, but I didn't know I was *so* incredibly bad.

No, no. Never mind. Don't put me in, coach. I don't want to go in. I'll just embarrass myself in front of my friend and my dad. I'll just sit here. No! I don't want to play anymore. Don't make me play! I'll just warm the bench. Unless I can't do *that* right either.

Maybe I *should* join the drama club. I can't be any worse at that, can I? At least I probably won't publicly humiliate myself anyway.

THE STAR

TODD

Doug! She wants me to wear this costume with *tights*. I really want this part, but I do not want to wear tights. No way! That's what ballerinas wear. It's just not a very masculine look for a guy. Well, what should I do?

If I just come out and say, "No way," she'll give the part to someone else. This is my *first* decent role ever. But I don't want to humiliate myself. I want girls to, like, swoon over me. I thought this was my chance. You saw how all the girls were hanging all over Paul last year when he was Romeo in *Romeo and Juliet*. I want that. But I can't pull this off. *Paul* got to wear pants!

Oh, Miss James, hi! No, no, nothing's wrong. Everything's great. Terrific. I love my costume. Love it! Thanks so much!

THE PATCH

MATTHEW

I wish I were a pirate. That they still existed. That's the life.
Being out on the high seas, robbing people, drinking, eating,
carousing . . . It sucks that you can't do that kind of stuff
anymore.

No way! It's not hard work. I'm talking about being a pirate,
not being in the army. Pirates are slobs. They do whatever
they want. You fight and go to islands where native girls
wear coconut shell tops. And if anyone gives you any problems, you make them walk the plank. I know a few people
I'd make walk the plank. I bet the world would be a better
place if you had to walk the plank instead of getting detention. You probably really learn your lesson if you're drifting
at sea for days on end.

So, what's close to being a pirate these days? You know, a
life where you can be lawless and where there are no limits
or restrictions? Politician? Can politicians wear eye patches?

SCIENCE FRICTION

TOPHER

Will you take some pictures of me for my website tonight? It's not weird. Please? I need help. I can't do it on my own. Look, just because it's not what you're into doesn't mean it's weird. It's perfectly normal. Lots of people are like this. It's not like I made this up. This is something people have done practically since the beginning of time. The spandex is an important part of it. It's critical. You can't be a *Star Trek* fan without the spandex suit. That's just the way it is. If you even watched one episode, you'd see what I mean. It's cool. You're just being really narrow-minded. *Star Trek* is one of the most awesome things to ever happen to TV ever. I *know* that if you watched it, you'd agree. You'd love *Deep Space Nine*; I know it. It has aliens and cyborgs and—

It's your loss. I don't even care. But get the camera. I'm going to put on my outfit. Do it! I'll tell Mom that you cheated on your bio test if you don't. Or I'll shoot you with my death ray. Either way, you're taking the website photos.

BEST FRIEND

BRUCE

I met this girl. You'd really like her. She's excellent. Beautiful.
Really beautiful. I can set you up if you want! Of course, I'd
do that for you. You're my friend. It's no problem.

Why don't I want her for myself? She's . . . she's not my type.
You know? Well, yeah, she's attractive. I'm just not . . . She
just seems like your type of girl. I want to help you out.
You're my best friend. I want the best for you.

I told you— OK. She's a little . . . bossy. But really pretty. I
asked her out because she looked so good, but she just . . .
talks a little more than I would like. But I think you'd like
her! I do! Why would I lie to you? I'm serious.

(Looking at his cell phone.) Oh God. That's her. Another text
message. I'll tell her about you, OK?

CHEAT

RICK

I didn't tell Mr. Walford. I didn't! Why would I? I'm going to get an A anyway. OK, OK! I would tell maybe if I knew. It's not fair to people like me who study. But I didn't know you were—that you cheated. I didn't see you. I didn't look at you. I was *thinking*. I was taking a test, remember? Why did you assume I was the one who ratted on you? Look, I don't like trouble. I'm not a confrontational person. I don't have any desire to start a fight. I'm not a fighting kind of guy, isn't that obvious? You're accusing the wrong person. You need to look elsewhere, guys. I'm not your man. I wouldn't do that.

(Quietly.) Well, of course, I told on them. I studied my butt off for that test!

I'M OK, YOU'RE SO-SO

NEIL

So, what flowers say, "Hey, you're OK. I like you, I guess"? That's what I'm looking for. Roses say love. I don't want those. She'll get the wrong idea. How about carnations? Too cheap? But I have no money. Shouldn't she just be happy I gave her flowers at all? I don't see the point of all this. Why do girls care so much about flowers? How come there are no gifts for guys? I get a flower, too? I don't want a flower. She should give me tickets to a baseball game or something. Look, I know I have to do this corsage thing since it's a prom, but she's not exactly my first pick; she's just who was left. Hey, maybe that's cruel, but I'm just being honest. If I'm too, like, romantic and stuff, she'll think I'm her boyfriend after this. I'm just going to get her pink carnations. It says, hey, I notice you're a girl, but I'm not that into you, OK?

Oh, God, I have to know what color her dress is, too? No, no. I'm done. This is too much work. I give up.

HIP-PY

JACK

Now I know you're going to laugh at me, but I'm asking this question totally seriously: Does my butt look big in this? Don't laugh! Something's wrong with these pants. What is it? I know I look like a girl, but I need a new pair of pants. Are you going to help me out or not? Just go away if you're not going to be helpful.

Stop laughing! I know they look terrible. I look fat. God, I do sound like a girl. But I need to upgrade my wardrobe. Everything I have is so, like, five years ago. I hate every single thing in my closet. Well, excuse me for wanting to look good. Is that such a crime? Then just arrest me, I guess.

ORDER

DARRYL

I can't find the remote! There's a game I need to watch now. Where the hell is it? I checked under the cushions. I even looked in the fridge 'cause that's where it was last time. Come on! It's kickoff time! Can you help me look? Where did you see it last? I've looked *everywhere*, Mom. If I don't find it . . .

No, I can't just turn on the TV manually. Then I can't adjust the volume! And I can't pause or replay. I have to find the remote!

Oh. Thanks! Where was it? On the TV? We never leave it there. Why was it there?

REINCARNATION

VAN

I think I'm my grandfather. My dad says I'm exactly like him. We look alike, and, I guess, we act alike, too. My grandfather was an engineer. I think I want to be one, too. What exactly do engineers do? I want to make bridges.

Do you believe in reincarnation? I do. I mean, why is my favorite color the same one as my granddad? But I don't think I was ever a bug. Or a girl. I don't get girls at all, and if I were a girl, I would, right? I think I was a king, too. I like telling people what to do. I never lived in Africa. I can't imagine what it's like to live in Africa. Or the desert. How can heat be dry?

No way, you weren't a king, too. You were like a farmer or something. I can see you being a farmer. I don't know why. Because of your hands. You look like you grew potatoes or something.

Listen, we can't both be kings. It's statistically impossible.

IN MY CAVE

EDWARD

Thinking is for losers. It makes me tired. And I hate working. I would love to sleep for a whole year. Or even a season, like a bear. Why can't we hibernate for the winter?

I am not a slob. Get out of my room. It *is* my room. I lived here first. I was born first. So it's my room. Go play outside or something. That's what kids are supposed to do.

Did you call me fat? You're gonna be sorry. I'm going to pull your head off and flush it down the toilet. I could, too. Don't try me. I'll do it. You better run.

I could catch you! If I felt like it.

LIFE CHOICES

NIEL

I could eat a horse. I never knew why people said that, until now. Why wasn't there any normal food at that wedding? Can we stop off for a burger? Please?

I'm never getting married. I could never live through the ceremony. That was *so* boring. And I hate smiling for so long.

I don't know why you say things like that, Mom. How do you know if I'll feel different later on? I bet I won't. It's not like I'm five. I'm old enough to know whether or not I want to get married. Everyone who gets married seems miserable. Except for you and Dad, of course. But most people. And why would you get married when you can just date? I don't see the point. It's just a piece of paper.

I don't need a wife to cook for me. I'll just go out to eat. Can we get that burger now?

LATE

SIMON

Can you help me? I'm supposed to be in the science building and I have no idea where that is. I'm late. Really late. Like the class is almost over. I accidentally turned my alarm off and went back to sleep. I have this roommate who feels like he needs to stay up 'til, like, four a.m. since he's not living at home anymore. It's sad.

So, wait. Where is this place? I feel so bad that I've started off on the wrong foot. Hope the teacher is cool about it. It's the first day, so she should be, right? But I hear that she's really tough. They even call her Das Bitch. She's German, I think. Which class? Oh, it's Bio 101. I'm a freshman. With Professor Frankel.

Oh! You're Professor Frankel? You seem really nice. Shouldn't you be in class, too? Wow, you're *really* late. I'm glad I'm not the only one.

FIRST DATE

ah, I did have a problem with drugs. But not anymore. I've been sober for six months now. I'm OK now. I'm different. I see the world totally differently. I'm not only clean, I'm super clean. Squeaky clean. I fast twice a year to clean out my system, you know, drinking only tea. I'm a vegetarian. The good thing about recovering from an addiction—well, not recovered completely, of course, but on the right path now—but the good thing is that you really appreciate life. I love being alive. I don't even put myself in a situation where I could be near drugs and alcohol. Jessica and I are going to have coffee. Well, I'll probably have green tea to be honest.

I promise I'll have her back home by, like, seven. I promise I'll totally respect her and your rules. The most dangerous thing she'll do tonight is get into my car. That came out wrong. I won't speed. Or, you know, touch her. Or . . . anything. Just us, getting coffee. Driving slow. So, where is she? Can we . . . go, sir?

PRESSURE

PHILIP

I don't know what I want to do for a living. Why should I.
I'm still a kid. I don't know why you're on about this all the
time. I'm young. I don't need to know what I want to do for
the rest of my life.

I do have focus in my life. I want to be a student. I want to
hang out with my friends and enjoy life. I want to get good
grades.

OK, fine. I'll choose what I want to be for the rest of my life
right now. When I was five, I wanted to be an astronaut. So
I'll go with that. I want to be a spaceman. OK, Dad? So, are
you going to send me to space camp this summer? You never
let me go when I was a kid, but now that it's my goal in life,
I think I'd better go, don't you?

TOO PRETTY

not a girl. I'm a boy. I just have long hair. I can't believe adults are so narrow-minded. Gender is not determined by hair alone. I don't have boobs. I'm not wearing makeup or a skirt or nail polish. Do you think girls with short hair look like boys? You do. Oh. Well, maybe you should rethink that. This is the twenty-first century. Anything goes nowadays. Fortunately for you, I'm not that sensitive. I like girls. Girls are pretty. They smell good. So if I seem like a girl to you, I guess that's a compliment. But other people might not be so nice about it. Once some lady asked my mom when the baby was due only she wasn't pregnant, and it made her really mad and hurt her feelings. So you should think before you speak. I guess things aren't the same as they were in your days. You grew up in, what? The forties or fifties? I guess guys had short hair then.

You grew up in the seventies? Well, then you have no excuse. I don't know what your problem is then.

BUMPY

JOEY

Mom, can I talk to you? In private, please? Mom, I don't
know exactly how to say this. No, I'm not on drugs. No
one's pregnant. No, Mom, wait. Listen! I don't want you to
wear my T-shirts anymore. They . . . they've got these bumps
in front, and they just won't go away. It's embarrassing. All
the guys say I have boobs. I'm sorry. Breasts.

I don't mean to . . . I mean, this isn't easy for me to talk
about, and you know I love you, and otherwise I wouldn't
care if you wore my stuff. You know what I'm saying, right?
You just stretch out the front of them. Maybe you could buy
your own shirts, OK? You deserve some, Mom. Go buy
yourself a T-shirt, Mom. I love you.

MY PEEPS

ICK

n I go to your party on Saturday? I don't know. You'll
have to talk to my people. My people, you know, my peeps,
Larry and Dylan. They're in charge of organizing my social
calendar. I like to delegate. My college applications are due in
six days, so I have to focus my time and energy. Dylan, do I
have a space free for a party on Saturday night? I have one
hour, including travel time. Where do you live? That's going
to be tough. That's, like, twenty minutes from my house.
Right, Larry? So that would only give me twenty minutes at
the party. Look, I'm thinking too much. I can't give this many
brain cells to this situation right now. I have to concentrate on
getting into an Ivy League. Sorry, but these details are just too
much for me. Take it up with Larry. I have to think about
what dead person I'd like to have dinner with. Bye.

PRIORITIES

JEROME

Tanya, you just don't get it. Sure, I have money for a car.
I don't want any old car. Any car won't do. Sure I want to b
more independent and take you out places. But wouldn't it
be better to go places in the kind of car that makes people
turn their heads and say, "Whoa!"

I know we don't see each other than much. And I've told you
that I'm sorry we have to take the bus to the movies. But I
want the best for you. You should be driven around in the
nicest car. And that's why I'm working so hard. Don't you
want to be the envy of every other girl in school? To have the
coolest boyfriend with the most amazing car?

No? Are you serious? I guess that's nice that you'd rather
spend time with me in a crappy car, but . . . are you serious?
That's just crazy. I'd prefer a guy with a great car, personally.

CRUSH

e's the thing. I've known you for a really long time, and ve been wanting to tell you something. That is, if you want to hear it. If you have somewhere to go or anything, that's OK, you can just go . . . . Well, the thing is, we've been friends for a while, and I think we get along really well. And there's something I've been wanting to tell you, but I've been afraid to tell you. I just didn't want to say it because I thought you might not want to hear it. It's not bad. Well, I don't think so. Maybe it is. It depends on your perspective. I mean, that how you feel about what I'm going to say depends on . . . Never mind. You don't want to hear it. It's really not important. It was silly. It's nothing. Really.

Well . . . OK. I was going to tell you that . . . I think . . . I kind of . . . I've known you for a long time and I think . . . uh . . . your eyes are two different sizes. Did you ever notice that? Becky? What? Are you mad at me?

MISTAKE #8,562

GEORGE

Ah, yes. My parents. They are supremely stupid. You wouldn't even believe it. Full of crap. My dad thinks he's always right, and my mom, well, she thinks she's always right, too. But the truth is that I'm always right, and they're too dumb to know it. It drives me crazy sometimes. They never let me do anything because they think I'm going to act like a dumb kid. I practically came out of the womb at twenty-five! I'm definitely the most mature person in my family.

Why do you have that weird look on your face? Does it shock you that I talk about my parents like that? It's the truth. They are clueless. They think I'm just some sweet, dumb kid. It's almost laughable! What is it? You look so . . . someone's behind me. Who is— Oh, Dad. How are you today? How was your day at work?

CELEBRATION

LIS

This is a great party. Even if I did have to wear a suit. I'm glad you made me come. I love you guys. Did you see all the shrimp over there? That's the most shrimp I ever saw in my life. And the chocolate fountain? I swear, I wanted to just stick my whole head in it. Looks awesome. No, I don't want to dance. I'm just gonna mingle. Oh! Oh! The grossest thing happened! I ate this thing off a tray that this waiter had, and then I asked the guy what it was. It was duck liver! I swear, I almost puked! I mean, who eats duck liver?

Oh. Am I being loud? I didn't know. No. No. I haven't been drinking. OK. OK. Maybe I had a few glasses of champagne. I don't know how many. They just keep refilling my glass. So it's hard to keep count. But it's just champagne. So, it's not like I'm drunk. I'm just happy. I love you guys! This party is awesome.

DAYTIME DIVA

MARCO

I want to be on a soap opera. I admit it! I love *All My Children* 'cause there's that hot blonde guy on it. Where do they film it? Is it in LA or New York? 'Cause I need to go there. I don't care about being an actor. I mean, I do, but I don't. Who cares if I'm good, you know what I mean? I don't want to study and be the best actor in the world. I just want to be on *All My Children*. I can do that kind of acting—crying, being pissed off, all that.

OK, if I'm being really honest, I want to be one of the divas. I want to wear fabulous dresses and furs and be a huge bitch! Don't you think that's one area daytime TV ought to go in? Isn't it about time that there was a big queen on TV? I mean seriously—Susan Lucci? I could break her in two with my pinky finger. Can't you just see me bitch slapping her?

SECOND CHAIR

HERB

I give up. I don't want to do this anymore. I just don't like it anymore.

I'm second chair. Second! I'm not second at anything. I won't accept second. So I give up. I don't want to do it anymore. I don't care if I've been working at this for ten years. I'll just practice on my own. Maybe I'll start my own orchestra. Can we practice in the garage? You can just park your car in the driveway, maybe, if that's OK. Or maybe I'll start a band. Forget the whole classical thing. Go off in another direction. Be a . . . a . . . pioneer or . . . something-breaker . . . what's the word? Anyhow, be original. So . . . that's what I'm going to do.

Oh, come on! Why can't I make any of my own decisions? I want to quit! Then Mr. Harper will be sorry he made me second chair. He'll be sorry when I'm a famous oboe-playing rock star.

THE CALL

JONAH

I'm going to call her. Right now. No, I'm not scared. It's no big deal. It's not like I've never done this before. I mean, I've done this lots of times. Three. Times. So I'm used to this. I just dial the number, and when she answers, I act all casual and say, "Hey, Karen. What's up? Want to hang out sometime?" I don't need to be more specific than that, right? That would be embarrassing, wouldn't it? If I came out and said, "Want to go on a date?" Because if I say only "let's hang out" then if she says no, I can be, like, "OK, fine," and she didn't *really* reject me because I didn't actually say it was a date. So then I can be like, "What's your problem?" if she tells people at school that I asked her out. Because I can be, like, "I didn't ask you out. I asked you to *hang* out. Two totally different things." Right?

Yeah. So. I'm going to call. Now. It's going to be cool. I think she'll say yes. She'll say yes, right? Yeah. So I'm dialing now. Maybe you should go into the next room. I don't want an audience.

(Picks up the phone. Dials.) Hey, Karen? Hi, this is Jonah. How are you? I was, uh, wondering if you might maybe want to go out on a date sometime?

HOTTIE

FINN

Ack! Give me some water, quick! Oh God! I'm dying!
What—what was that? What is in this stuff? I don't know—
Oh, man, I need more water. My throat is burning. My poor
tongue. There was, like, some kind of hot pepper in this!
Really hot. The water isn't helping. I'm on fire! This really
hurts.

Waiter? Waiter? Please pay attention to me. He's ignoring
me. Doesn't he realize I'm dying? If he ignores me for one
more second . . . don't give him a tip. If I die, sue them, OK?
(Standing up.) Excuse me? Help? I'm not going to sit down.
I'm in pain. I have to get relief! Waiter! My mouth is on fire.
What can I do? Help me! What was in that food?

He thinks I'm crazy. I don't care. I can't die here. I knew I
never should have tried Indian food.

TOP CAT

TOM

Why did I get a C? I worked really hard on this paper. Really hard. It's at least a B paper. You hardly even wrote any comments on it! What's wrong with it? Well, I'm sorry if this sounds rude, I don't mean to be, but how is that supposed to help me? "It's not as good as some other people's work." How am I supposed to improve with a comment like that? It's not very . . . constructive. I'm sorry, but I can't walk away with a grade like this. I stayed up late for three days working on it. I did all the research; I did everything you asked. And I just don't understand why I didn't do better. I want to get an A in this class. Can't you give me any more points? Any tips for getting better? I've never gotten a C in my whole life. I was an honor student at my old school. No disrespect intended, but are you *sure* this is a C paper? Maybe you got my paper mixed up with someone else's. This is a really good paper. Could you just give me some more comments?

Go away. Go away? That's your comment? I hate this school. I hate everything. But most of all, I hate that guy who sold me this paper. What a waste of money!

A.M. RITUALS

PETER

I won't stop singing in the shower. I like singing in the shower. What's wrong with my singing? I think it's good. I don't care if you don't like it. I enjoy it. It's not a "racket." That's my rapping. I rap, too. I'm getting good, too! Maybe I'll even make a career of it. Just you see. Then you'll be sorry because I won't give you any of my millions.

Stop laughing. It's not funny. You are such a jerk. So what are you going to do with your life that's so great? A corporate executive. That's so exciting. So exciting I could fall asleep right here and now. Grow an imagination! Until you get an imagination, I cannot respect your taste in music. My singing is *great*.

THE HAUNTING

JONATHAN

We can't live here any more. I can't live here any more. This place is spooky. There are ghosts here. I'm serious! I wouldn't say it if I wasn't serious! I've been quiet about this for a few days now. But every night when I try to go to sleep, I hear footsteps in the attic. It's freaking me out. There's no other explanation! Maybe we can get our old house back. Call them now. Maybe we can sue the real estate agency, too, for not telling us this place is haunted. Probably some family just like us were massacred, murdered right here. I'm freaking myself out! But this place feels wrong. I feel like someone's watching me now. I didn't even believe in ghosts until now!

Dad's been putting boxes in the attic? Yeah, but has he been doing it at, like, midnight? He has? Oh. So, then . . . I guess it's not haunted. Maybe. I still feel like someone's watching me. I swear it! Let's just go back home. It's really the safest thing. Better to be safe than sorry, right?

PSYCHIC

DAVID

Oh, yeah. That's me. I'm the kid who talks to dead people. It's for real. Do you want me to prove it? OK, fine. But it'll cost you. Don't walk away. I'm telling you, it's for real. Try me. Tell you what. I'll only charge you five bucks.

OK. I'm getting someone whose name starts with a J . . . John? Jerry? Jason? Do you know anyone who's passed with these names? No? A "J" name? Jeremy? Jenny? Janine? Jamie? Ah-ha! See? George. That has a J sound. And that person is your . . . grandfather. Uncle. Uncle! Uncle George. And he wants to tell you that he's proud of you. How well you're doing in school. You get C's? Well, he's saying that he got D's. I think you'll find if you talk to your relatives, they'll back me up on this. Uncle George was not the smartest guy on the block. He graduated from Princeton? Yeah, but his family bought him in. Just ask your family. No? He lived in a trailer growing up? There must be someone nearby who's interfering.

(Standing and yelling.) Does anyone here have a stupid Uncle George? Anyone? *(Sitting.)* OK, fine. Here's your five dollars back. I'm just having a bad day. That's all.

THAT GUY

HUGH

Um, I don't know how to tell you this, Dad, but . . . Well, I found this picture the other day when I was looking for my eighth-grade graduation picture, and it was of Mom and a guy. Not you. Some guy. And she was . . . He had his arm around her, and they looked like they were friendly. Maybe even in love. It was kind of upsetting. No, no, Dad. I didn't want to do this, but maybe I should show you. I just keep looking at it. They look so happy, see? And they're, like, all over each other. Her arm is around him. And they have bathing suits on. It's, like, gross and wrong. This picture doesn't look that old. It only looks a few years old. And I didn't want to show you because I was afraid you and Mom would break up and get divorced, and you'd be sad, but I just had to tell you.

That's her cousin? She's in love with her cousin? I don't know, Dad, they look *really* happy here. I guess I can see that *maybe* I could be wrong, but I've been looking at it . . . well, never mind. She *likes* her cousin? Weird.

MOM'S FRIEND

MEL

Cook dinner? Are you serious? Can't I just order out?
There's nothing to eat here! I don't know how to cook. I
don't *like* to cook. Why are you going out? There's *nothing*
to eat here. Why can't I just get a pizza? If we have to watch
the money, why are you going out to dinner? I'm not being
smart. I'm just saying it makes no sense. You get to go out
on a date, and I'm stuck here with nothing to eat. Not even
mac and cheese. My life is totally not fair. I'm not ungrateful!
I'm *hungry*. I want *pizza*.

Thanks, Mom! You're the best. I promise I'll clean up after I
eat. I hope he buys you a really nice meal. If there's anything
left over, will you bring it home for me?

OLD-FASHIONED

BRENDON

I really don't understand the obsession with the Internet. It seems like a sneaky way to get kids to do research and homework to me. E-mail is overrated. I don't need to be in touch with friends every minute of the day. Why would I want to e-mail you at night? I see you at school.

MySpace? Don't even get me started. What do I care if some kid in California wants to be my "friend"? I figure everyone on that site is a pedophile anyhow. Watch the news! Jeez, it's so obvious. Everyone on the Net is pretty much a pedophile. Unless I really know someone, I assume anyone on the Net is a freak. I'm not being paranoid. I'm being smart. And I am never, ever going to work at the White House. If the Internet pedophiles don't get you, the politicians will.

DELAY

MARTY

No, no! It's not funny. Don't joke about that. Shut up! Are you— You're not just saying that are you? Because it would not be funny at all.

I was just going to call her! I know I've been talking about it for a week. I needed to get, well . . . I needed to get my thoughts together. I couldn't figure out what to say.

I know it's not that hard! "Do you want to go to the prom with me." It *seems* easy, but this is Sabrina. I have such an image of the prom. I want it to be perfect. The perfect girl, the perfect tux, the perfect after-prom— We were going to go to the beach! I had it all planned out. I saved up for the limo! How could she be going with someone else?

I hate myself. Why didn't I ask her sooner? Now I'm going to be alone forever. This was my one shot at happiness.

Hey—do you know if Nicole Blakely is going with anyone?

THE MAN

OTTO

Look at this, Jenny. Come here. I've got something to show you that will BLOW YOUR MIND.

(Pointing to his chest.) See? No? Right there. There! The hair! I got my first chest hair, OK? This is important. Don't you know what this means? I'm a *man*. A man! It's official. So . . . I just thought you'd want to know. In case, you know, whatever.

I don't know! I just thought maybe you'd . . . I don't know. You just don't get it. This is important. You should be impressed.

No, I'm not going to be all hairy like a gorilla now. I'm going to have just the right amount of hair. You like smooth-chested guys? Hairless? What are you a pervert or something? I'm just saying that only kids are hairless. You might want to reconsider that and trade up for a *man*. Just a suggestion.

THE BABY

CARLOS

That's OK. I don't need to. Really. Oh, well . . .

(Holds his arms as if cradling a baby.) You really should take her back. I don't think . . . I'm just a kid. This isn't safe. I feel like I'm going to drop her. Am I doing this right?

OK, OK. I just need to calm down. She's crying! She's crying! What did I do? Did I do that? Did I hurt her? You should take her back. No, she's not OK. I upset her. I don't know what to do. Walk around? *(Starts walking.)* It' not work— Oh. OK. *(Relaxes.)* Yeah, maybe she does like me. That was easy. Yeah, we're cool, aren't we, Bella? Oh, Jesus, she's crying again. Take her! Take her! I can't take the pressure!

TRAINING

TERRY

So. Come on over here, ma'am. Let's see what your fitness level is. Um, well, I'm eighteen, ma'am. Why don't you get on this bike, and we'll see how you're doing. Uh, yeah, I'm still in high school. But I know my stuff. My dad owns this gym. Don't worry; you're in good hands.

I'm getting the feeling you don't want to do this, ma'am. Is it my age? I swear, I wouldn't have you do anything that's not good for you. I really know what I'm doing. But if you really want someone else to work with you, I'll go to the office to see who's available, ma'am.

Oh. Is that it? Well, sure. I can call you Patty. No problem.

So now, what's the problem? No one likes to exercise, Patty. Well, practically no one. But if you want to lose twenty pounds, you're going to have to get on this bike.

HULK

ALEC

(Loud and aggressive, in a deep voice.) You better watch your back! The Rooster is gonna rearrange your face! Tonight at seven—in my backyard—the fight of the century! The Rooster versus Spider Boy! Not to be missed. There's gonna be blood. He's gonna wish he was never born!

(Shouting, but in a more normal voice.) No, Mom! It's nothing! I'm just practicing! *(Turning to the right.)* How did that sound, Nick? What's wrong with being the Rooster? I've always been the Rooster. So what sounds tougher? The Hulk? It's been taken. The Blob?!? Makes me sound fat. Chunk is that weird kid in *The Goonies*. Vicious is the name you'd give to a guard dog. This is a pointless conversation. I'm the Rooster. And a rooster can definitely beat a Spider Boy. Please! Roosters can step on spiders, or peck them to death.

So do you think people will come? This is going to be the start of something big for the Rooster. *(Back into wrestler voice.)* The world better look out! The Rooster is coming!!

(Yelling in normal voice.) No, Mom. Still just joking around. Everything's OK!

ROTTEN

HAL

Mom, look at this refrigerator. I'm not kidding. This is unbelievable. And you complain about being overweight. You've got cookies and ice cream and cheese— Yes, cheese is bad for you. You cannot just go on a diet every few months and be healthy. It's sick. I'm so sick of females talking about how they're fat while they eat brownies and Diet Coke. It's so stupid.

Look, you don't need a hundred diet books. I'll tell you what's healthy. Vegetables and fruit! Chicken! Normal food! It's not that hard.

Well, sure, I eat chips and stuff. But I'm not overweight.

What are you doing? Why are you throwing that stuff out? It's new! It's good! Just because you're going to start getting healthy, that doesn't mean I have to, too! Never mind what I said before. Take the chips out of the trash, Mom!

DATE NUMBER TWO

GRANT

So, wussup? How's it going? Good, good! That's good. *(Beat.)* I had a really great time last time we went out. It was good. Yeah. Really good. It's good to see you again! This is going to be good. Fun. Good. Yeah. *(Beat.)* So! What are you going to order? Grilled cheese is an excellent selection. I like cheese. Everyone likes cheese, right? Cheese is good. Are you getting fries? *Love* fries. I'm gonna get fries. Probably a cheeseburger, too. Love that cheese! Excellent. Yeah. Yeah. So.

(Beat.)

So—Rachel . . . uh . . . So! How's it going? I asked you that? Oh. OK. Well—

Are you serious? I don't have to come up with conversation? You know, it's weird. When I see you in school, saw you in school before we started this going out together thing, I thought it was really easy to talk to you. I didn't even think about it. Now . . . I don't know . . . So, I can relax? Really? You don't mind? Man, that is such a relief!

AB-SOLUTELY

ALF

I've been working out for three months now. What's it going to take to get a muscle? Look at my abs. Exactly! You don't want to. Neither do I. No matter what I do, I'm coated in blubber. So why do I bother?

Well, yeah, sure I'm stronger. Here's the thing. I feel like if I lifted weights every day for a year I'd probably look a little different. But would I look like I want to? Probably not. I'm just genetically made to be a blob. Why fight it? Plus, even if I somehow managed to keep this up for a year, can I keep it up for a lifetime? No way. This is killing me. It's boring. No one ever talks about that. It is so boring to exercise!

No. I'm done. I'm just gonna suck in my gut whenever I'm around Diane Garko. Maybe that'll be enough.

DE-CONSTRUCTIVE

FREDDY

I. Have not. Slept. In three days! I. Can't! GO ON! I never realized what not sleeping does to a person. I always thought insomniacs were whiners. Or lucky even. Because they have extra hours in the day to do stuff. But this is unbelievable. I can't think straight. I can barely move. I keep tripping over stuff. Honestly, this is dumb, but I almost feel like—well . . . this is between us, OK, Matt? It's like I want to cry sometimes. Because I'm just so freakin' tired. It's like I'm going crazy. I'm not myself. I don't know what to do!

I called the police, and they said there's nothing we can do. It's a government thing, so they can do whatever the hell they want. Can you believe that?! Makes me want to blow the road up. That will show them. Maybe I will. Or something like that. I'll screw up everything for them. See how they like that! Who will be miserable then? Ha! I like this idea!

Oh yeah. I guess then there will be even more construction. I'm doomed!

POSSESSED

NEIL

Dad, can I talk to you? This is embarrassing. Never mind.
Forget it. I'm going to do my homework. No. It's nothing.
Really. It's just that . . . I can't do my homework. I can't do
anything. Well . . . I have this problem. I have an obsession, I
guess. I think all the time about this one thing. No, not that.
Well . . . not exactly that. I mean, yes and no. OK, OK!
It's . . . cheerleaders. I have this thing for cheerleaders.
Oh, man, this is so embarrassing.

OK, I know I can talk to you, it's just that . . . Fine. I, like,
daydream all day, all the time, about dating a cheerleader,
watching cheerleaders rehearse, cheerleaders really digging
me. I can't think about anything else! Whenever I have to do
my math homework, or whatever, I open the book and see—
cheerleaders. I can't focus on anything else. I want to stop
but . . .

There's nothing I can do? Just try harder to focus? I don't
think *everyone* has this problem. Otherwise, how would the
world run? How would anyone do their jobs? How would
that kid Jeff get A-pluses in all his classes?

Well, thanks, I guess. Listen, don't tell Mom about this, Dad.
Please. I couldn't handle that.

GOTTA GO

GAVIN

Ew, Anthony, I am not going to help you in the bathroom.
Mom! Anthony has to go to the bathroom! Mom? I am not
helping you. Because it's gross. I know you have to go. I
heard you. Go find Mom. She went to the store? Oh, man.
Look, you're going to have to learn to do this stuff—

Oh no you didn't. Oh, gross. I can't believe you just did that.
Don't move! You're just spreading it all over the house.
Maybe you should still be in diapers. I am *not* cleaning this
up. Well, unbuttoning your pants is part of going to the
bathroom, Anthony. If you can't do that—OK, look, I'm
sorry, but I can't help you—

I can't believe I'm doing this. Oh, God, this is disgusting.
Mom, why aren't you here? OK. Anthony, don't move. I'm—
uck—I'm going to help. You are going to owe me for the rest
of your life now. I hope you know that.

ILLOGICAL

LES

(Confident.) OK, so you get that problem, right? Let's look at cosigns. You're doing better. You are. You're kinda getting it. Don't stress. You have to think you're going to get it. OK. Let's look at, uh, number twelve. Where do you think you should start? Think about— *(Freezes in fear.)*

(In a squeaky voice.) Uh, Janine? Um, whatever. Janine, can you come over here? I, uh, there's a situation. It's, uh—shhh! Look over there. Do you see? The spider! The spider! On the wall! Shhh! Don't move! What should we do? Are you scared of—

Oh. You killed it. *(Relieved.)* Oh my God, you are so brave. I swear, spiders—I know this makes no sense, but—I can't believe you just killed it! You're my hero, Janine!

ROCK AND ROLL

JAY

Hey, Mike, let's trash this hotel room. Like rock stars. Come on, what can they do? It's not even a hotel room. It's a motel room. We'll be out of here before they even know what happened. We're leaving tomorrow. What can they do? Come on. Worst case scenario, we'll get detention. Or suspended. What's so bad about being suspended, anyway? You get out of school. What could be better? It's like you're actually being rewarded.

Do it. Come on. Throw the chair. I dare you. Do it!

(Beat.)

Oh my God. The wall—I can't believe the wall broke! The hole is huge! We are getting in so much trouble, Mike. Why did you do that? I can't believe you listened to me!

THE AUTHOR

Kristen Dabrowski is an actress, writer, acting teacher, and director. She received her MFA from the Oxford School of Drama in Oxford, England. The actor's life has taken her all over the United States and England. Her other books, published by Smith and Kraus, include *The Ultimate Monologue Book for Middle School Actors Volume I: 111 One-Minute Monologues*, *The Ultimate Audition Book for Teens Volume III: 111 One-Minute Monologues*, the *10+ play* series, the *Teens Speak* series, and *Twenty 10-Minute Plays for Teens Volume 1*. Currently, she lives in the world's smallest apartment in New York City. You can contact the author at monologuemadness@yahoo.com.